VIRTUAL FIELD TRIPS

THE
NATIONAL MALL
A MyReportLinks.com Book

Kate Robinson

MyReportLinks.com Books
an imprint of

 Enslow Publishers, Inc.
Box 398, 40 Industrial Road
Berkeley Heights, NJ 07922
USA

MyReportLinks.com Books, an imprint of Enslow Publishers, Inc. MyReportLinks® is a registered trademark of Enslow Publishers, Inc.

Library of Congress Cataloging-in-Publication Data

Robinson, Kate.
  The National Mall / Kate Robinson.
    p. cm. — (Virtual field trips)
  Includes bibliographical references and index.
  ISBN 0-7660-5222-2
  1. Mall, The (Washington, D.C.)—Juvenile literature. 2. Washington (D.C.)—Buildings, structures, etc.—Juvenile literature. 3. Washington (D.C.)—History—Juvenile literature. I. Title. II. Series.
  F203.5.M2R63 2005
  975.3—dc22
                                        2004009001

Printed in the United States of America

10 9 8 7 6 5 4 3 2 1

To Our Readers:
Through the purchase of this book, you and your library gain access to the Report Links that specifically back up this book.
The Publisher will provide access to the Report Links that back up this book and will keep these Report Links up to date on **www.myreportlinks.com** for five years from the book's first publication date.
We have done our best to make sure all Internet addresses in this book were active and appropriate when we went to press. However, the author and the Publisher have no control over, and assume no liability for, the material available on those Internet sites or on other Web sites they may link to.
The usage of the MyReportLinks.com Books Web site is subject to the terms and conditions stated on the Usage Policy Statement on **www.myreportlinks.com**.
A password may be required to access the Report Links that back up this book. The password is found on the bottom of page 4 of this book.
Any comments or suggestions can be sent by e-mail to comments@myreportlinks.com or to the address on the back cover.

Photo Credits: AP/Wide World Photos, p. 12; © 1995 Smithsonian Institution, p. 11; © 1999 PhotoDisc, pp. 1, 9, 21, 26, 28, 32, 34, 36, 41; © 2004 National Coalition to Save Our Mall, Inc., p. 15; © 2004 National Gallery of Art, Washington D.C., p. 16; © Corel Corporation, pp. 1, 3, 23, 25, 42; Enslow Publishers, Inc., p. 17; Mural by Allyn Cox, p. 38; MyReportLinks.com Books, p. 4; National Capital Planning Commission, p. 20; National Park Service, p. 13; Reproduced from the *Dictionary of American Portraits,* published by Dover Publications, Inc., in 1967, p. 18; The White House, p. 39; United States Senate, p. 30.

Cover Photo: © 1995 PhotoDisc (Lincoln statue); © Corel Corporation (background and statue of soldier).

Cover Description: On the lower left is the statue of Lincoln that is located in the Lincoln Memorial. The background image is of the Vietnam Veterans Memorial, with the Washington Monument in the distance. The image of the soldier on top is also part of the Vietnam Veterans Memorial.

Report Links 4

The National Mall Facts 9

1 A Grand Avenue 10

2 A New Federal City 13

3 America's Front Yard 18

4 Jenkins Hill 28

5 A Presidential Palace 34

6 The Changing Face of the
Federal District 40

Glossary 43

Chapter Notes 44

Further Reading 47

Index 48

MyReportLinks.com Books
Great Books, Great Links, Great for Research!

The Internet sites listed on the next four pages can save you hours of research time. These Internet sites—we call them "Report Links"—are constantly changing, but we keep them up to date on our Web site.

Give it a try! Type http://www.myreportlinks.com into your browser, click on the series title, then the book title, and scroll down to the Report Links listed for this book.

The Report Links will bring you to great source documents, photographs, and illustrations. MyReportLinks.com Books save you time, feature Report Links that are kept up to date, and make report writing easier than ever!

Please see "To Our Readers" on the copyright page for important information about this book, the MyReportLinks.com Web site, and the Report Links that back up this book.

Please enter **FTN1405** if asked for a password.

Report Links

The Internet sites described below can be accessed at http://www.myreportlinks.com

*EDITOR'S CHOICE

▶The National Mall
Approved by George Washington, the National Mall was designed to be the centerpiece for the capital of the world's greatest nation. Visited by millions of people each year, the Mall offers you a chance to visit history up close.

*EDITOR'S CHOICE

▶Creation of the National Mall
Read the history of the National Mall, the Washington Monument, and West Potomac Park. A time line of important dates for the National Mall is also provided.

*EDITOR'S CHOICE

▶Virtual Tour of the National Mall
View panoramic shots of National Mall landmarks, such as the Smithsonian Castle, Capitol building, and Lincoln Memorial. Descriptions of each of them are given.

*EDITOR'S CHOICE

▶The National Mall
Take a short tour of the National Mall, and learn some of its history and geography. Take the scramble quiz at the end of the tour to test your knowledge.

*EDITOR'S CHOICE

▶Camera Over Washington
Photographers from the Smithsonian Institution provide aerial shots of Washington's National Mall from Capitol Hill to the Potomac River. Click on the images to enlarge them.

*EDITOR'S CHOICE

▶National Mall
Read about some of the planners and architects for various sites on the National Mall and the history of the Mall's development.

Report Links

▶ **Franklin Delano Roosevelt Memorial**

President Franklin D. Roosevelt led the country through the Great Depression and created a new era for the United States. President for four terms, he was passionate about inspiring hope and overcoming catastrophe.

▶ **Historical Tour of the White House**

Click on the different rooms of the White House to view interior photographs and read the histories provided. You will also see a variety of paintings, portraits, china patterns, and historical furniture on the tour.

▶ **History of Planning in Washington**

Pierre Charles L'Enfant was a French architect and urban designer. His plan for Washington, D.C., emphasized parks and grand buildings. Many others built on his plan over the years.

▶ **Korean War Veterans Memorial**

Located on the National Mall in Washington, D.C., the Korean War Veterans Memorial is made up of nineteen life-size soldiers, a wall of faces copied from photographs of veterans, and a low stone wall listing the twenty-two countries that made up the United Nations forces in Korea.

▶ **The L'Enfant Plan**

L'Enfant was hired by George Washington to design a basic plan for Washington, D.C., and the area now known as the National Mall. Learn more about L'Enfant at this Web site.

▶ **Lincoln Memorial**

The Lincoln Memorial is located on the National Mall and is visited by millions of people each year. Learn more about its construction and history.

▶ **Major Memorials, Washington, D.C.**

This is an excellent map of the monuments and memorials of the National Mall in Washington, D.C. Print it out, and use it for your school projects.

▶ **Monuments Quiz**

What do you know about the National Mall in Washington, D.C.? Are you familiar with the important national memorials and monuments that are found on the Mall? Test your knowledge at this Web site.

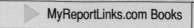
Report Links

The Internet sites described below can be accessed at
http://www.myreportlinks.com

▶ **National Coalition to Save Our Mall**

The National Coalition to Save Our Mall is fighting to prevent over-development of the National Mall. This Web site is a great resource for materials on the National Mall, including its history, great moments, chronicles, photographs, and more.

▶ **The National Gallery of Art**

In 1941, Franklin D. Roosevelt accepted the National Gallery of Art, located on the National Mall, on behalf of the nation. The building and its collection of art was a gift to the country from industrialist Andrew W. Mellon.

▶ **National Mall**

The National Mall is the site of many important landmarks, memorials, and buildings. Read how the area evolved from farmland and marsh to one of the most visited places on the planet.

▶ **National Mall Walking Tour, Washington, D.C.**

You will learn a lot of history when you take this *National Geographic* virtual tour of the National Mall. A map of the area is included.

▶ **Smithsonian Institution**

James Smithson, a British scientist, left his entire estate to America so the country could create a place that would aid in the spread of knowledge. This became the Smithsonian Institution. Links to all Smithsonian museums, including those located on the National Mall, are provided.

▶ **Smithsonian Institution Building, The Castle**

The Castle is the chief information center for the Smithsonian Institution and acts as its administrative headquarters. This building is a popular tourist destination.

▶ **Smithsonian Museums On and Near the National Mall**

This map displays the Smithsonian museums located on the National Mall in Washington, D.C. Also provided are pointers to other important landmarks in the area, such as the Capitol building and the Washington Monument.

▶ **Thomas Jefferson Memorial**

The memorial to Thomas Jefferson, the third president of the United States and author of the Declaration of Independence, is one of the most visited in Washington, D.C. Learn more about this founding father.

Report Links

The Internet sites described below can be accessed at http://www.myreportlinks.com

▶**U.S. Capitol Virtual Tour**

View panoramic scenes on this interactive multimedia tour of the Capitol building. Historical information on the rooms and furnishings is provided, as are additional photographs to increase your understanding.

▶**United States Holocaust Memorial Museum**

Located a few blocks from the National Mall, the Holocaust Museum is dedicated to the memory of those who died on the orders of Nazi Germany. The museum is a research center and archive with a mission to educate the world about the tragedy and suffering of the Holocaust.

▶**Vietnam Veterans Memorial**

Located on the National Mall, the Vietnam Veterans Memorial has a wall of names listing everyone who died fighting or went missing during the Vietnam War. The Three Servicemen Statue and Flagpole and the Vietnam Women's Memorial are also nearby.

▶**Virtual Tour of Washington, D.C.**

Learn about the District of Columbia and some of its famous sites by taking this virtual tour of the landmarks on the National Mall. A great map of Washington, D.C., is also included.

▶**The Virtual Tour of Washington, D.C.**

Learn the history of important Washington landmarks and view art exhibitions as you take this virtual tour. Many museums, monuments, memorials, and government buildings are included.

▶**Washington, D.C.**

You will see the major memorials and monuments, as well as important buildings, such as the Capitol, White House, and Treasury Department, at this Web site.

▶**Washington, D.C., Sightseeing Map**

This map shows many of the major landmarks on the National Mall. Clicking on individual links brings you to information and history pages for each site. Learn more about the capital city of America.

▶**Washington Monument**

Located on the National Mall, the Washington Monument symbolizes the powerful and elegant man it was built to honor. You will learn the history of both the man and the monument, as well as the importance of Washington's legacy.

When George Washington convinced Virginia and Maryland landowners to sell property to build the new federal city, they agreed they would receive no money for land that became avenues and streets. The landowners were astounded when they found L'Enfant's design had streets 100 to 110 feet wide, avenues 160 feet wide, one grand avenue 400 feet wide and a mile long, and a Mall nearly 2 miles long.

George Washington was the only United States president who did not live in the White House. However, he oversaw the White House design. Construction began in 1792 and was completed after Washington's death in 1799.

After British scientist James Smithson's entire fortune was donated to the U.S. government for establishing the Smithsonian Institution, 105 bags filled with gold British sovereigns (gold coins) were carried to the United States aboard the ship *Mediator*.

The House of Representatives met temporarily in an oval-shaped, brick room constructed at the future site of the south wing of the Capitol during 1801. It was nicknamed "the oven" because representatives said it was always hot.

In 1844, Samuel Morse sent the world's first long-distance telegraph message from an unknown location in the Capitol basement somewhere around the chamber of the Supreme Court.

It takes nearly six hundred gallons of white paint to cover the outside walls of the White House.

The east and west interior walls of the Washington Monument are lined with 193 memorial and two descriptive stones donated by American states, foreign governments, private citizens, fraternal organizations, nineteenth-century trade organizations, Sunday schools, fire departments, and a ladies' group.

The elevator in the Washington Monument takes 70 seconds to reach the 500-foot level.

Kite flying was illegal on the Washington Monument grounds until 1967, the year the curator of the National Air and Space Museum founded the annual Smithsonian Kite Festival. Soaring kites are limited to 550 feet, lower than the 555-foot monument.

The Jefferson Memorial. ▷

A Grand Avenue

When President George Washington asked Major Pierre L'Enfant to design the monumental center of Washington, D.C., both men imagined a "grand avenue" honoring American ideals and history. What they may or may not have imagined was that the National Mall would become a stage for some of the most important events in modern history.

▶ A National Stage

Freedom, justice, and other ideals inspire people to gather on the National Mall. Dedicated Americans feel these gatherings are fine examples of democracy in action. The Lincoln Memorial, especially, has been the site of many stirring civil rights demonstrations.[1]

The American civil rights movement reached a turning point during the summer of 1963. African Americans, other people of color, and their white supporters called for an end to school segregation and job and housing discrimination. The smaller local protests of previous years grew into a major revolution. That summer, the movement was on the minds of everyone from ordinary people to leaders in the highest levels of government.[2]

A. Philip Randolph, an African-American union leader, proposed a march on Washington, D.C., to dramatize this struggle.[3] Bayard Rustin, another African-American political activist and tireless supporter of the civil rights movement, organized the "March on Washington for Jobs and Freedom."[4]

Churches, labor organizations, students, celebrities, and thousands of ordinary citizens supported the march. People from

http://photo2.si.edu/aerialdc/mall3.gif - Microsoft Internet Explorer

File Edit View Favorites Tools Help

Address http://photo2.si.edu/aerialdc/mall3.gif ▼ 🔁Go Links »

© 1993 Smithsonian Institution

Done · Internet

▲ *An aerial view of the National Mall.*

every state in the union streamed into Washington, D.C. On August 28, 1963, Dr. Martin Luther King, Jr., delivered his famous "I Have a Dream" speech on the steps of the Lincoln Memorial before 250,000 people at the end of the march. The event touched the conscience of the nation and became the single most moving demonstration for freedom and justice in America's history.[5]

Another famous event that happened at the Lincoln Memorial was the 1939 Easter Sunday concert by Marian Anderson. She sang to seventy-five thousand people gathered on the grounds. The African-American performer had been denied the right to sing at Constitution Hall in Washington, D.C.[6]

 Martin Luther King, Jr., salutes the crowd before his "I Have A Dream" speech. He is standing on the steps of the Lincoln Memorial.

▶ Recent Demonstrations

Many important and moving demonstrations continue to take place in "America's front yard." On October 16, 1995, an estimated 878,587 African-American men gathered on the National Mall for the Million Man March. Leaders of the march asked participants to "take responsibility for their lives and families, and commit to stopping the scourges of drugs, violence and unemployment." The huge crowd stretched from the foot of the Capitol to the base of the Washington Monument.[7]

By early 2000, all major gun-control legislation in Congress had been stalled for a year, frustrating President Clinton and other supporters. Many people were upset by the 1999 Columbine High School killings in Littleton, Colorado. Two teenagers had been able to buy weapons. With those weapons they killed fifteen students, including themselves, at school.[8] Five hundred thousand people demonstrated for tougher gun laws at the Million Mom March on Mother's Day 2000. The Capitol building was a striking backdrop for the huge gathering.[9]

Chapter 2

A New Federal City

Washington, D.C., is more than an ordinary city. It is a federal district rich in drama and history. It was the first capital city in the world established by law and designed before being built.[1] Washington, D.C., grew slowly over many years as America's bold experiment in democracy took form.

D.C. stands for the District of Columbia. The District of Columbia is not part of a state like other American cities. It was

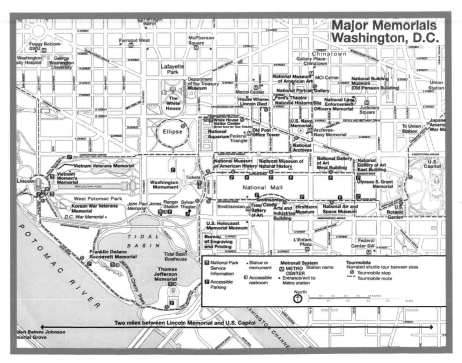

▲ This map shows the layout of the National Mall from the Lincoln Memorial to the U.S. Capitol building.

built on the Territory of Columbia, at the fork of the Potomac and Anacostia rivers between the states of Maryland and Virginia.

▶ A Capital Location

After the Revolutionary War (1775–83), the people of the young republic argued about a permanent site for the capital city. Northerners wanted Philadelphia or New York to be the capital of the United States. Both were comfortable places to live and work. Congress had held sessions in the two cities. New York, though, was considered too far north to be a good permanent capital. News traveled only as quickly as people could travel by boat or horseback. Getting news to the Southern states from New York would take a long time. Philadelphia was a better choice. Many people assumed the new government would stay there because it was the leading city of the nation.[2]

Southerners had many reasons for placing the capital near Southern states. Many Southerners and members of the Anti-federalist party wanted the new nation to have fewer cities and more farms. Their interest was in wealth based on land. Northerners living in cities and members of the Federalist party were interested in wealth based on trade. There was a big difference between these lifestyles. George Washington believed that farmers and businessmen could live in peace together.[3] Still, conflict and rivalry grew between the North and South. Many Northerners were not happy with the slave trade in the South. Congress discussed the location of the capital for seven years.[4]

On April 6, 1789, General George Washington of Virginia was elected president of the United States. Secretary of State Thomas Jefferson, Secretary of the Treasury Alexander Hamilton, and Congressman James Madison had conflicting ideas about establishing the federal government and the new capital. They had many debates about these issues. They arrived at a compromise over a dinner at Jefferson's New York residence in May 1790.[5] The new capital would be placed on the Potomac River,

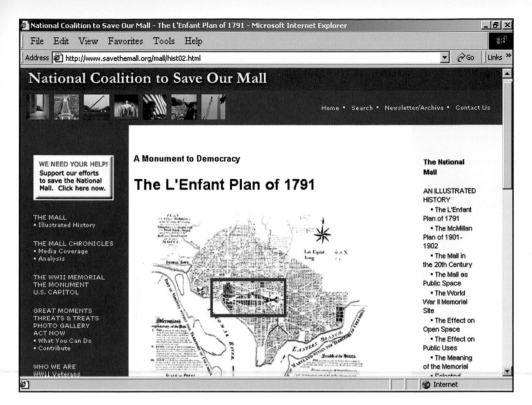

National Coalition to Save Our Mall – The L'Enfant Plan of 1791 – Microsoft Internet Explorer

File   Edit   View   Favorites   Tools   Help

Address http://www.savethemall.org/mall/hist02.html

National Coalition to Save Our Mall

Home • Search • Newsletter/Archive • Contact Us

WE NEED YOUR HELP!
Support our efforts
to save the National
Mall. Click here now.

THE MALL
• Illustrated History

THE MALL CHRONICLES
• Media Coverage
• Analysis

THE WWII MEMORIAL
THE MONUMENT
U.S. CAPITOL

GREAT MOMENTS
THREATS & TREATS
PHOTO GALLERY
ACT NOW
• What You Can Do
• Contribute

WHO WE ARE
WWII Veterans

A Monument to Democracy

The L'Enfant Plan of 1791

The National
Mall

AN ILLUSTRATED
HISTORY
• The L'Enfant
Plan of 1791
• The McMillan
Plan of 1901–
1902
• The Mall in
the 20th Century
• The Mall as
Public Space
• The World
War II Memorial
Site
• The Effect on
Open Space
• The Effect on
Public Uses
• The Meaning
of the Memorial
• Selected

Internet

▲ *When planning the layout of Washington, D.C., designer Pierre Charles L'Enfant envisioned the National Mall to be a "place of general resort." He wanted this open space to shorten the symbolic distance between the Capitol, where the legislature meets, and the White House.*

just between the Northern and Southern states. Congress settled down and met in Philadelphia for the next ten years, until the capital city was ready.

The Ten-Mile Square

In January 1791, President Washington picked the site for the new capital. His choice allowed the district to include the busy river towns of Alexandria, Virginia, and Georgetown, Maryland.[6] He had long favored this location because he felt it would be a good area for commerce.[7] Washington felt his decision would satisfy all the states' interests.

Washington chose Pierre Charles L'Enfant, an enthusiastic French engineer, to plan and lay out the city. L'Enfant had fought alongside the colonists during the Revolutionary War. His sketches of soldiers had impressed Washington during the Revolutionary War.

President Washington chose Major Andrew Ellicott to survey the federal district. At the same time, L'Enfant worked on his plans and started the project. Benjamin Banneker, a friend of the Ellicott family, helped him. Banneker, a freeborn African American, was a skilled astronomer and surveyor. Washington, L'Enfant, Ellicott, and Banneker spent a lot of time in June 1791 riding over the hilly tract of land on the Potomac River.[8]

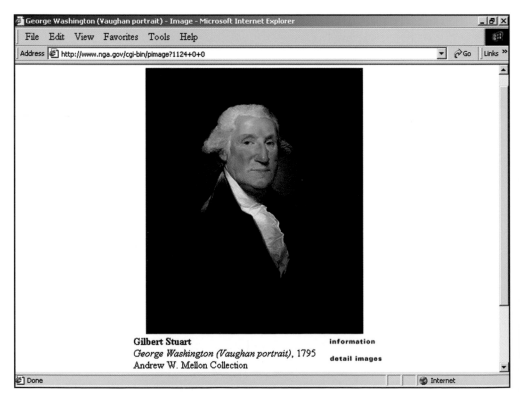

George Washington (Vaughan portrait) - Image - Microsoft Internet Explorer

File   Edit   View   Favorites   Tools   Help

Address http://www.nga.gov/cgi-bin/pimage?1124+0+0

Gilbert Stuart
George Washington (Vaughan portrait), 1795
Andrew W. Mellon Collection

information

detail images

Done   Internet

▲ The National Gallery of Art, located on the National Mall, contains this Gilbert Stuart portrait of George Washington. Stuart painted this in 1795 while Washington was serving his second presidential term in the country's former capital, Philadelphia, Pennsylvania.

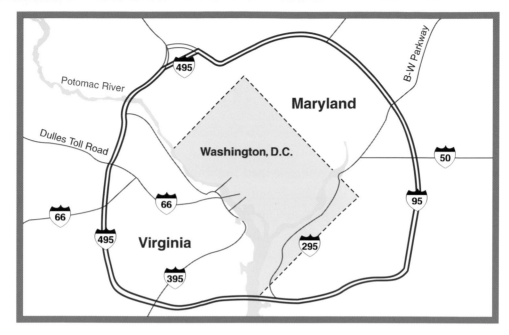

▲ *Washington, D.C., is located along the banks of the Potomac River. It is nestled between Maryland to the north and Virginia to the south.*

Washington appointed three unpaid commissioners to oversee the project. Judge Thomas Johnson, David Stuart, and Daniel Carroll told the president they had agreed to call the city Washington in honor of the president. The district was named Columbia in honor of Christopher Columbus, the famous explorer.

The ten-mile-square District of Columbia was surrounded by woods, brush, and marshes in 1791. It was not much more than a village. Three thousand people lived among cornfields and construction sites. There were few roads to link it with the rest of the nation.

In May 1800, 130 federal employees moved from Philadelphia. Neither the "President's House," as Washington called it before his death in 1799, nor the Capitol building was finished. President John Adams, the Supreme Court, and Congress arrived in the District of Columbia during November 1800. Washington, D.C., was finally the official seat of the United States government.

Chapter 3

America's Front Yard

Pierre L'Enfant imagined building a city "worthy of a great empire." He designed broad avenues angling across a grid of streets. But L'Enfant did not begin work with the usual survey lines and street grids. First he selected sites for buildings and a mall—a long, wide grassy strip of land also called a "common" in the eighteenth century.[1]

▶ Heart of the Federal District

The Mall became the foundation of L'Enfant's design. He called it a "Grand Avenue."[2] In his plan it stretched 400 feet wide and more than a mile long. It ran westward from Capitol Hill and ended with a monument honoring George Washington.

L'Enfant's open design allowed contact between the federal government and the people. The executive, legislative, and judicial branches

◀ *The National Mall was the centerpiece of Pierre Charles L'Enfant's design when he was drawing out plans for a capital city. This engraving is one of the few images of L'Enfant that exist.*

▶ 18 ◀

of government would be housed in three separate buildings. This illustrated the idea of separate and balanced powers. The "Congress House"—L'Enfant's name for the Capitol building—sat on Jenkins Hill overlooking the Potomac River. Broad and long Pennsylvania Avenue linked Congress with the "Presidential Palace" a mile away. The long National Mall also connected the Capitol grounds to the president's home. Both were symbols of the lines of communication between the president and Congress. The judicial branch sat between the President's House and Congress, showing that the federal courts stood uninfluenced by the other two branches of government.[3]

L'Enfant would not hurry or take advice from anyone except the president. His way of thinking and working upset the commissioners and local landowners. Poor conditions and lack of money slowed work.[4] President Washington had Thomas Jefferson remove L'Enfant from his job in 1792. The idealistic architect worked on the federal city only one year. He was not recognized or rewarded for his work in his lifetime.[5]

L'Enfant's Vision Revived

Andrew Ellicott and Benjamin Banneker took up where Pierre L'Enfant left off. They made very few changes to his plan. Money was scarce, and not many people wanted to live there.[6] Eventually, L'Enfant's plans were almost forgotten. Grazed by wandering sheep, cows, pigs, and geese, public markets were held on the Mall during the nineteenth century.[7] It held Union Army troop encampments through the Civil War. Later, the Baltimore and Potomac Railroad laid tracks and built a depot on the Mall.

In 1901, Congress revived L'Enfant's plan for the capital city. Senator James McMillan headed a Senate commission that made decisions about redesigning Washington, D.C. The commission included some of the most well-known architects of the time, namely Daniel H. Burnham and Frederick Law Olmsted, Jr. The McMillan Plan removed the railroad tracks and depot on the Mall.

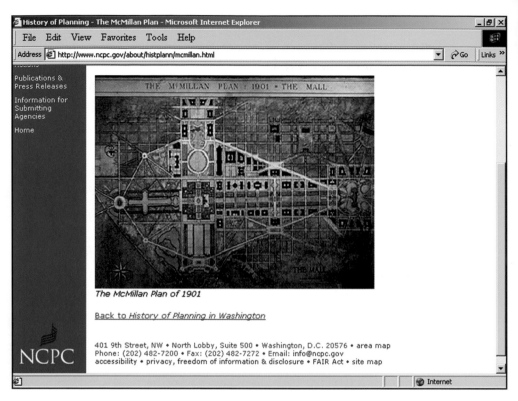

History of Planning - The McMillan Plan - Microsoft Internet Explorer

File   Edit   View   Favorites   Tools   Help

Address | http://www.ncpc.gov/about/histplann/mcmillan.html

Publications &
Press Releases

Information for
Submitting
Agencies

Home

THE McMILLAN PLAN : 1901 · THE MALL

The McMillan Plan of 1901

Back to *History of Planning in Washington*

NCPC

401 9th Street, NW • North Lobby, Suite 500 • Washington, D.C. 20576 • area map
Phone: (202) 482-7200 • Fax: (202) 482-7272 • Email: info@ncpc.gov
accessibility • privacy, freedom of information & disclosure • FAIR Act • site map

Senator James McMillan's 1901 plan changed the National Mall to reflect the connection between the Washington Monument and the Capitol.

It called for building the Lincoln and Jefferson memorials. It extended the Mall westward to the banks of the Potomac River.[8]

A Tribute to Washington

The first memorial on the Mall would honor George Washington. L'Enfant's 1791 plan included a place for Washington's statue. Washington approved the plan, but the statue was never built. In the 1830s, Congress agreed that sculptor Horatio Greenough would create a statue of George Washington to be placed in the Capitol building. He posed Washington like a bare-chested Greek god. The statue shocked the American public. They said it looked like Washington was "climbing out of his bath." Within a few years, the statue was moved from the Capitol Rotunda to the Capitol grounds. It has been displayed in the National Museum of American History since 1964.

Many people felt that design of a monument took too long. They started the Washington National Monument Society in 1833. This organization opened a monument design contest to American artists in 1836. Robert Mills, the Washington, D.C., architect of public buildings, won the contest. Mills's design was styled like a Greek temple. It had a tall obelisk on top of a circular building. In the mid-1840s, the design changed to a simple Egyptian-style obelisk to save money.

A monument site was not chosen until 1848. Then the federal district held the grandest Fourth of July ceremony anyone remembered. Twenty thousand people gathered at the Mall. They watched Grand Mason Benjamin French place the cornerstone of the monument. French wore George Washington's Masonic apron and blue sash from the 1793 Capitol cornerstone ceremony.[9]

The "Know-Nothing" party upset construction in 1854 when they took control of the Monument

The Washington Monument and the reflecting pool. There had been plans to honor George Washington with a monument as early as 1791, but after many delays, the monument was finally dedicated in February 1885.

Society. Know-Nothing workers added 26 feet of second-rate stone to the monument over the next three years. After the Know-Nothing party fell apart, the Monument Society raised money for the project until the November 1860 election. Then people's attention turned to President Abraham Lincoln and the issue of slavery. In 1861, the Southern states left the Union. The Civil War began. The unfinished monument became a symbol of the divided nation.[10] It was still not completed in 1874, when Mark Twain said the Washington Monument looked like "a factory chimney with the top broken off."[11]

Work did not start again until 1876. Engineers laid a new foundation. They took down the Know-Nothings' inferior blocks.[12] In December 1884, the U.S. Army Corps of Engineers topped the monument with a capstone and aluminum tip.[13] A ceremony dedicated the monument a day before Washington's birthday in February 1885. Construction of the slender, white shaft spanned thirty-six years and eleven presidential administrations. It is still the world's tallest freestanding stone structure at 555 feet, 5⅛ inches tall.[14]

▶ West Potomac Park

In 1914, ground was broken in West Potomac Park for a memorial to America's sixteenth president, Abraham Lincoln. Architect Henry Bacon, sculptor Daniel Chester French, and artist Jules Guerin were chosen to design the Lincoln Memorial. Bacon's design is like a Greek temple in remembrance of the origins of democracy. It also represents the unity of the Northern and Southern states and has thirty-six columns for the thirty-six states that were in the Union when Lincoln died in 1865. Lincoln's two great speeches, the Gettysburg Address and his Second Inaugural, are engraved on the monument's north and south walls. French's statue of Lincoln inside the memorial gazes eastward across the Reflecting Pool at the Washington Monument.

The long Reflecting Pool and smaller, oval-shaped Rainbow Pool connecting the Washington Monument and the Lincoln

People visit the Vietnam Veterans Memorial to pay tribute to the soldiers that gave their lives during the Vietnam War. The memorial was dedicated on November 13, 1982.

Memorial were designed by Frederick Law Olmsted, Jr. Both monuments' images can be seen in the water of the Reflecting Pool. The pools were completed soon after the Lincoln Memorial dedication in 1922.

The Vietnam Veterans Memorial stands a few thousand feet from the Lincoln Memorial. It honors the American men and women of the armed forces who served in the Vietnam War (1964–75). Maya Lin, a young Chinese-American architectural student, designed the long, black granite wall engraved with all the names of Americans who died in Vietnam. Her design was unpopular at first, but it is now considered one of the world's great war memorials. Some people think it has helped heal the national rift caused by the war.[15]

Just across the Reflecting Pool from the Vietnam Veterans Memorial is the Korean War Veterans Memorial. It honors the nearly 2 million American men and women who served in the Korean War between 1950 and 1953. It has a black granite wall. On it is a mural etched with photographs representing veterans of all races and ethnic groups. One of the most interesting features of the memorial is a group of nineteen stainless-steel statues depicting a variety of armed services soldiers. There are fifteen statues of Army men, two Marines, one Navy medic, and an Air Force observer.

The National World War II Memorial is the newest memorial on the National Mall. It stands at the east end of the Reflecting Pool. Rhode Island architect Friedrich St. Florian's design was selected in a national design contest. He worked the Rainbow Pool into the memorial design. The memorial honors the 16 million men and women who served during America's war effort and the generation who supported them at home from 1941 to 1945. It is a reminder of the strength of people united in a just cause.[16]

The Sylvan Theater is an open-air stage on the Washington Monument grounds. Plays, military band concerts, and other entertainment are presented there during warm weather months.

The Tidal Basin

The Franklin Delano Roosevelt Memorial stands in West Potomac Park along the famous Cherry Tree Walk between the Tidal Basin and the Potomac River. Shade trees, gardens, water-falls, and pools grace the four outdoor galleries representing Roosevelt's four terms in office (1933–45). They include a sculpture depicting the hope and despair of the Americans during the Great Depression and World War II.[17]

When President Franklin D. Roosevelt came to Washington, D.C. in 1932, he was disappointed there was no memorial to President Thomas Jefferson. Jefferson is remembered as the author of the Declaration of Independence and a brilliant man of many talents. Roosevelt wanted a monument that showed all aspects of his character. In 1934, a government commission asked architect John Russell Pope to submit a design. Many people were upset that other designers were not considered and wanted a design contest. Even so, Pope's plans of a dome design that Jefferson had used for his home, Monticello, went forward. The design was based on the Pantheon in Rome, which Jefferson believed to be the perfect example of a circular building. The memorial is a reminder of all the ideals that Jefferson wanted for his country: independence, equality, and education.[18]

▲ *The Tidal Basin offers some of the most beautiful views of Washington, D.C., and the National Mall area. The Jefferson Memorial is shown here on the right of the photo. The Washington Monument is on the left.*

Nearly four thousand cherry trees grow near the Jefferson Memorial at the Tidal Basin, in East Potomac Park, and on the Washington Monument grounds. Thousands of visitors tour the National Mall in springtime to see the masses of pink and white cherry blossoms. The original trees were a gift from Japan to the United States in 1912.[19] About one hundred twenty-five original trees are still alive, including the first two planted.[20]

▷ The Smithsonian Institution and the East Mall

A wealthy British scientist died in 1829. He left his entire fortune to the United States government. James Smithson's will stated his money should be used to found "an establishment for the increase and diffusion of knowledge" named after him.[21] Whether to accept the gift or not was a matter of controversy for the next three years.[22] Legislators, scholars, and scientists debated about the best use of Smithson's money. President James K. Polk signed a bill honoring Smithson's wishes on August 10, 1846. It called for an institution dedicated to research and public education.[23]

The cornerstone for the Smithsonian "Castle" was laid on May 1, 1847. This building was the original Smithsonian Institution.

The Smithsonian is the largest museum complex in the world. Ten of the Smithsonian Institution's museums and art galleries have been built along the Mall. Smithsonian museums and galleries exhibit American and international history, art, culture, science, and technology. Millions of visitors enjoy film, theater, and music programs and several festivals there each year.

The National Museum of the American Indian (NMAI) on the National Mall opened in 2004, filling the Mall's last available space. NMAI began with a welcome center that opened after a traditional native blessing in June 2001.[24] NMAI is the fifteenth Smithsonian museum and the first national museum dedicated to American Indian arts, history, and material culture.[25]

George Washington suggested creating a national garden as early as 1796. In 1820, Congress authorized the creation of the

▲ The Smithsonian Castle housed the original Smithsonian Institution and museum. Today, the Castle is mainly used as offices, but it is still one of the most interesting buildings along the National Mall.

U.S. Botanic Garden. It was maintained in many places in Washington, D.C., until 1933. Then it was moved to its current location at the eastern end of the Mall. The garden has thousands of species of plants from many environments. The plants are used for exhibition, study, and exchange with other institutions. The U.S. Botanic Garden sponsors a wide variety of exhibits, workshops, and programs throughout the year.

The Ulysses S. Grant Monument stands on the eastern end of the National Mall, near the Smithsonian museums and the Capitol building. It honors the Union commander of the Union forces in the Civil War, who later became the eighteenth president. The bronze General Grant sits on his warhorse, the largest equestrian statue in the world.[26]

America's Front Yard Today

Many people feel the National Mall is too crowded. Others think there is room for more memorials. Two proposed memorials may honor African-American patriots of the Revolutionary War and the work of Dr. Martin Luther King, Jr. They will be built only if enough money is gathered beforehand and Congress continues to authorize the projects.

Americans are trying to balance the need for security with the need for freedom after the worst terrorist attacks in America's history. On September 11, 2001, a hijacked United Airlines aircraft was crashed into the Pentagon near Washington, D.C. Another passenger flight crash-landed in Pennsylvania. It is thought that the intended target was the Capitol building. Since that day, security has been increased on the National Mall. The National Capital Planning Commission is working on guidelines for better security measures. There is a controversial plan for a tunnel to the Washington Monument. If approved, the tunnel would become the only access to the monument. Many engineers and citizens oppose the project. They feel it is important to have complete access to landmarks important to American history.[27]

Jenkins Hill

Pierre L'Enfant and George Washington walked the site of the new federal city on a June day in 1791. L'Enfant said the enchanting view from a rise overlooking the Potomac River was "a pedestal waiting for a monument." He wanted the new nation's "Congress House" built on the rise known as Jenkins Hill.[1]

L'Enfant expected to design the city's public buildings, but he lost his job before he could produce a design for the Capitol building.[2] Secretary of State Thomas Jefferson persuaded President Washington to select public building designs through holding contests. A committee consisting of the three district commissioners announced the design contests for the "Congress House" and the "President's House" in March 1792. Winners would receive five

▲ A view of the Capitol building from the west. The Senate building is on the left and the House of Representatives building is on the right.

hundred dollars and a city lot. Jefferson wrote the newspaper announcement, but there were few professional architects in the new nation. The judging committee was unhappy with the entries. They debated the "Congress House" designs for many weeks. George Washington politely called five of the designs "a credit to architecture in an infant republic."[3]

A thirty-year-old amateur architect wanted to send an entry to the Capitol design contest. Although the deadline had passed three months before, the commissioners were interested in physician William Thornton. They told Thornton they would gladly accept his submission. Dr. Thornton gave his design to President Washington in January 1793. Washington admired Thornton's design for its "grandeur, simplicity, and beauty of the exterior."

▷ Capitol Conflicts

Everyone was happy with Thornton's design except Stephen Hallet. The French-born architect's design had been in first place before Thornton submitted his entry. Hallet received a compensation prize of five hundred dollars, and the commissioners placed Hallet in charge of Capitol construction. Thornton had no practical skills in building. This started the first of many conflicts in planning and building the United States Capitol.[4]

President Washington formally approved Dr. Thornton's design. Workmen started digging the foundations for the "Congress House" in August 1793. On September 18, a parade made its way from the "President's House" to Jenkins Hill. The mansion was just a half-dug foundation on this sunny autumn day. Many side streets disappeared into thick woodland. Scattered houses and tree stumps littered the scene. Goose Creek, renamed the Tiber, had no bridge. The parade halted so Washington and other officials could scramble across the creek on a fallen log or from rock to rock. The procession reached the top of the rise and surrounded a large, squared stone. President Washington laid the Capitol cornerstone over an engraved, silver plate. The Masonic ceremony ended with prayers, an artillery volley, and a picnic of barbecued ox.[5]

Like all projects in the federal district, the Capitol construction proved slow and expensive. Stonecutters expected high wages to work away from home. Sandstone and heavy materials had to be delivered on boats. The commissioners stopped work on the south wing, meant for the House of Representatives, in August 1796. They aimed limited resources at the north wing. A finished Senate Chamber for the entire Congress seemed better than an unfinished building. When the government arrived in the federal district in 1800, the north wing of the Capitol held the House of Representatives, the Senate, the Supreme Court, the Library of Congress, a district court, and a variety of clerks.[6]

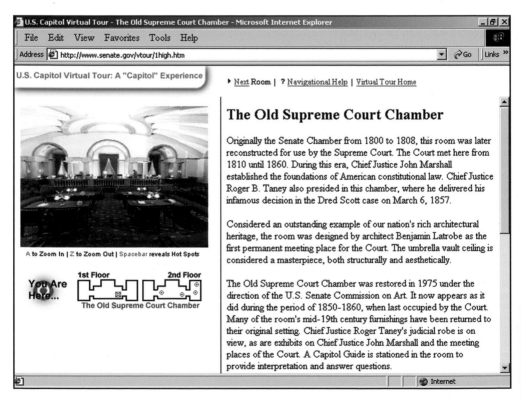

U.S. Capitol Virtual Tour - The Old Supreme Court Chamber - Microsoft Internet Explorer

File   Edit   View   Favorites   Tools   Help

Address http://www.senate.gov/vtour/1high.htm

U.S. Capitol Virtual Tour: A "Capitol" Experience

▶ Next Room | ? Navigational Help | Virtual Tour Home

The Old Supreme Court Chamber

Originally the Senate Chamber from 1800 to 1808, this room was later reconstructed for use by the Supreme Court. The Court met here from 1810 until 1860. During this era, Chief Justice John Marshall established the foundations of American constitutional law. Chief Justice Roger B. Taney also presided in this chamber, where he delivered his infamous decision in the Dred Scott case on March 6, 1857.

Considered an outstanding example of our nation's rich architectural heritage, the room was designed by architect Benjamin Latrobe as the first permanent meeting place for the Court. The umbrella vault ceiling is considered a masterpiece, both structurally and aesthetically.

The Old Supreme Court Chamber was restored in 1975 under the direction of the U.S. Senate Commission on Art. It now appears as it did during the period of 1850-1860, when last occupied by the Court. Many of the room's mid-19th century furnishings have been returned to their original setting. Chief Justice Roger Taney's judicial robe is on view, as are exhibits on Chief Justice John Marshall and the meeting places of the Court. A Capitol Guide is stationed in the room to provide interpretation and answer questions.

A to Zoom In | Z to Zoom Out | Spacebar reveals Hot Spots

You Are Here...   1st Floor   2nd Floor
The Old Supreme Court Chamber

▲ From 1800 until 1808, this room in the Capitol building served as the Senate Chamber. After undergoing reconstruction, the room was changed to the Supreme Court Chamber, where the judicial body met from 1810 until 1860.

Conflict grew between Thornton and Hallet. Thornton wanted his design intact. Hallet declared Thornton's plan expensive and time-consuming.[7] Hallet tried to introduce small changes from his own second-place design into the project. A confrontation caused Hallet's dismissal in 1794. George Hadfield became the next superintendent of construction in 1795. He was dismissed in 1798. James Hoban became the third architect to work on the Capitol. He had designed and directed work on the "President's House." Work progressed quickly. Congress moved from Philadelphia into the nearly completed wing in 1800.

In 1803, President Thomas Jefferson chose Benjamin Latrobe to be America's chief architect and engineer. Jefferson and Latrobe made a brilliant team. Jefferson sketched his own designs of the Capitol and took a keen interest in the project.[8]

Like others before him, Latrobe found some faults in Thornton's plan. He recognized that the Capitol's south wing needed more than a House Chamber. The members of the House of Representatives needed offices and committee rooms. Thornton was not happy with the changes, but Jefferson heartily approved them.[9] Since 1802, the House had met in an oval-shaped room in a temporary brick building thrown up on the wing's foundation. Latrobe and his crews tore down the temporary building and began construction of the South wing. The House met for the next three years in their original quarters in the north wing. After Latrobe completed the House wing, he renovated the Senate wing, which had a leaky roof and cracking walls. He raised the floor in the high chamber, making two rooms. In 1810, the Senate returned to the top room of their old chamber. The Supreme Court moved into the chamber below.

▶ A Temple of Justice

L'Enfant's plan proposed a separate building for the Supreme Court. Like Congress, the Court convened in many places until the federal district was established.[10] When the United States government settled in Washington, D.C., the Supreme Court had no building. Congress allowed the Court to use a room in the Capitol. Sometimes construction forced the Justices to move. They met in nearby homes and taverns as they had after a 1789 Act of Congress required Court Justices to preside over circuit courts. For nearly 146 years, the Court conducted business in the Old Supreme Court Chamber inside the north wing. Supreme Court Justices made the earliest landmark decisions from these crowded quarters under the Senate.

The Supreme Court building was one of the last important government buildings constructed. President William Howard Taft lobbied for a separate Court building in 1912 and when he became Chief Justice in 1921. Architect Cass Gilbert submitted a Greek or Roman temple design in 1929. At a cornerstone laying of the cross-shaped building on October 13, 1932, Chief Justice Charles Evans Hughes said, "The Republic endures, and this is the symbol of its faith." The building was completed in 1935.[11]

▲ *The Supreme Court did not have its own building until 1935. That was its 146th year of existence. The building (shown here) was worth the wait, as it is considered to be one of the most beautiful government buildings.*

▶ Today's Capitol and Supreme Court Buildings

Congress and the Capitol complex have grown and changed together. The Capitol has been burned and rebuilt, extended, and restored. The dome changed greatly from Thornton's original design. Charles Bulfinch, the first American-born architect to work in Washington, D.C., took over construction of the Capitol in 1818. Bulfinch rebuilt the Capitol after the British burned it in August 1814. He added a copper-sheathed dome higher than Thornton's original.

Congress set aside money for expansion of the Capitol in September 1850. The larger building needed a bigger dome. Architect-engineer Thomas Walter designed the tiered dome we see today. Walter traveled in Europe and sketched many domed buildings. He used his notes to design the Capitol dome. It was constructed of cast iron because it is inexpensive, fire resistant, and castable in complex designs. The tall dome is the most striking feature of the United States Capitol.[12]

Work on the Capitol stopped for nearly a year after the Civil War (1861–65) began, even though President Abraham Lincoln wanted construction done while the war raged. The capitol building housed a Union hospital, barracks, and bakery in 1861 and 1862. Walter's dome was finished late in 1863. Sculptor Thomas Crawford's statue *Freedom* crowned the building. Workmen bolted it together over five cold, windy days in November and December and hoisted it in pieces atop the Capitol dome. A huge crowd watched from the Capitol Plaza while President Lincoln lay in bed with a fever.[13]

The Capitol and the Supreme Court buildings are works of art. Their stately architecture reflects democratic order and ideals that date back to Ancient Greece. Both contain many famous paintings and sculptures. Many people appreciate the Supreme Court and Capitol buildings as memorials celebrating the creativity and determination of the American people.[14]

Chapter 5 ▶

A Presidential Palace

Pierre L'Enfant thought that rulers of great countries should live in palaces. His "President's Palace" was five times the size of today's White House. The European style plan placed the mansion on 80 acres of formal gardens. Terraces and fountains stretched all the way to the Potomac River. L'Enfant sketched his idea and President Washington approved it.[1] Washington agreed that presidents of the United States should live in style. He wanted federal district public buildings of "size, form, and elegance."[2]

Washington preferred an English country manor made of stone. In his imagination it was as big as politics would allow. Most Americans wanted a simple home. A president was not a king or an emperor. Washington finally agreed with what the

▲ When plans for the White House were first drawn up, Washington called it the "President's House." It is believed that people began calling it the White House in 1807.

people wanted. The "President's House"—the name he liked best—should suit the small nation. Remodeling could come later when the United States had become a great country.[3]

The district commissioners set up a design contest for the President's House in March 1792. In April, they selected a Scottish mason named Collen Williamson as overseer of the project. Dublin-trained architect and builder James Hoban won the design contest by July. He modeled his design on a duke's Irish palace. Hoban was appointed to build the President's House. Washington suggested Hoban leave out the third story from his design.[4]

Construction Begins

George Washington picked the site of the President's House. He moved it higher on the ridge to the west where it stands today. In August 1792, he drove stakes in the ground at the site. Williamson, a group of Masonic lodge members, stonecutters, and the district commissioners laid the cornerstone on October 12, 1792. Washington's duties kept him in Philadelphia.

There was trouble ahead even though the cornerstone was placed in a grand ceremony. The big project needed many workers. Skilled stonecutters and masons were scarce. Slaves could be rented cheaply from their owners. Twenty-five African-American slaves were hired to do the work. Williamson began the project by training slaves to quarry stone. They were eventually replaced by Scottish apprentices. Costs soared. It was decided only the bottom floor of the house would be solid stone. The rest of the walls would be brick with stone facing.[5]

The President's House was built of Aquia Creek sandstone. It had a rosy color when dry and a grayish color after a rain. Sandstone is soft and must be sealed by painting or whitewashing. The walls of the President's House were first whitewashed in 1797.[6] It was nicknamed the "White House" as early as 1802.[7]

In March 1797, George Washington's presidential term ended. He and his family headed home to Mount Vernon. He

▲ *A view of the rear of the White House and its gardens. James Monroe was the first president to live in the White House after it had been rebuilt from the damage done during the War of 1812.*

visited the President's House construction site one last time. Two oval rooms that Washington liked were on the first and second floors. The roof was not finished, and the yard was littered with workmen's shacks and construction supplies. The floors were laid of wood instead of the marble that Washington wanted. As he passed toward the Potomac River, he stopped in front of the house. Workmen saluted him with shouts and cannon blasts. This was the first celebration at the new President's House.[8]

▷ America's Grandest House

The President's House earned the title of America's largest house by 1797 and would hold that title for the next seventy years. President John Adams and his wife, Abigail, moved into the unfinished mansion in November 1800. Only six rooms of the new mansion were completed. A jumble of construction materials and mud covered the grounds. Twelve fireplaces were stoked to keep the house warm. There were few servants to cut firewood from the surrounding woods and no well. Water had to be carried from Franklin Park—a half mile away. Abigail Adams used the huge East Room only to dry laundry. There were no fences or clotheslines outdoors.[9]

After a hotly contested election, Adams's vice president became president. Thomas Jefferson lived at a boardinghouse after the government moved to Washington, D.C. On March 4, 1801, Jefferson dressed in simple clothes. He walked from his boardinghouse to the Capitol for his inauguration. Afterward, he walked back to the boardinghouse with congressmen and friends. He ate dinner at the common table with the other boarders. Some people felt Jefferson took his belief in democracy too far by taking his regular place at the table.[10]

Jefferson moved into the house two weeks after his inauguration and remodeled. He added a well, two indoor toilets, a fence, and a wine cellar to the mansion.[11]

War of 1812

The United States and Great Britain clashed and started the War of 1812 (1812–15) in June. The British boarded American ships, kidnapped British-born sailors, and tried to interfere with American trade. News that the British landed in Maryland spread like wildfire on August 21, 1814. President James Madison left the White House to join forces at the front. He said good-bye to his wife, Dolley, and asked her to protect important private and public papers. The next day, Madison wrote her two letters urging her to keep her carriage ready to take her out of the city. Dolley almost filled a carriage with trunks and linen bags of important papers.[12]

Dolley refused to be rushed and ignored pleas to leave the city. At noon on August 24, she sat at her desk and wrote to her sister as the boom of cannon fire echoed from the fields of Bladensburg. She did not leave until her servant cut Gilbert Stuart's large portrait of George Washington out of its frame.

That night, Admiral George Cockburn captured Washington, D.C. The British set fire to most of the public buildings, including the President's House. Admiral Cockburn and his men enjoyed the dinner spread by servants before everyone fled. The fires burned until a violent summer rainstorm quenched them. The President's House became a soggy shell with soot marks on its outer walls.

The attack on Washington, D.C., discouraged many Americans. They talked of moving the capital city farther west. President Madison ordered the President's House rebuilt. On February 15, Congress passed a bill that set aside money for reconstruction of public buildings. James Hoban was called back to Washington, D.C. He spent a year gathering materials and hiring workmen. Dozens of workmen labored twelve hours a day for the next year. When President James Monroe was inaugurated on March 4, 1817, the roof was in place and the floors were laid. The walls were painted white that summer. People started calling the mansion "White House" once again.[13]

▶ A Changing White House

The White House carries the mark of every president since Washington. Each president has had new ideas and a personal style. Some have been involved in the design and construction decisions. Others have requested additions or purchased furnishings and works of art. Changing

◀ This mural, painted by Allyn Cox, was called The Burning of the Capitol. This is the artist's conception of how things may have looked when the British burned the Capitol building and White House in August 1814.

The Green Room - Microsoft Internet Explorer

File   Edit   View   Favorites   Tools   Help

Address http://www.whitehouse.gov/history/whtour/photoessay/green.html   Go   Links »

Home > History & Tours > Online Tour of the White House

Tours
- Tour in Person
- Tour On-Line

Presidents & First Ladies
- Presidents
- First Ladies
- Kid Bios
- Kids Quiz

White House
- Art
- Eisenhower Executive Office Building
- Facts
- Life in the White House
- Room Art and Furnishings

Events & Traditions
- African-American History Month
- Presidents' Day
- Baseball
- Grounds and Garden
- Easter Egg Roll
- Christmas & Holidays
- State of the Union

The State and Public Rooms of the White House

Thomas Jefferson first used the Green Room as a dining room and covered the floor with canvas painted green. Today, elegant paintings of various people and scenes decorate the walls of the Green Room.

◄ BACK   NEXT ►

Internet

Since 1800, the Green Room has been used as a "Common Dining Room" as intended by James Hoban, as well as a sitting room, guest bedroom, card room, and more.

needs and technology have created many alterations in the building. Public rooms on the first floor of the White House still contain many treasures of national history and culture. The White House endures as a public museum and a symbol of the spirit of America.

Chapter 6 ▶

The Changing Face of the Federal District

When George Washington picked the federal district site, a few African Americans may have lived there. It is doubtful any were free. Virginia law required that freed slaves leave the state within six months. Maryland did not encourage them to live there. None owned property or a home inside the district. In 1792, Benjamin Banneker wrote to Thomas Jefferson describing his race as "long labored under abuse . . . and considered rather brutish, than as human, and scarcely capable of mental endowments." Banneker proved to the world that black men were as intelligent as white men.[1]

▶ A Capital Dilemma

The cities of Washington, Georgetown, and Alexandria were the main centers of the slave trade. Many people in the new nation felt slavery should stop. People opposed to slavery, called abolitionists, disliked the fact that there were slave pens near federal buildings and monuments. It seemed wrong to buy and sell people in a nation dedicated to freedom. But Congress ignored the problem. Congress looked at slavery laws in Maryland and Virginia in the early 1790s and adopted similar laws in the District of Columbia.[2]

Slaves often came to Washington, D.C., with their owners. They were rented out to work on public building projects or sold on the auction block. Ninety African-American slaves worked on the Capitol building project in 1798. By 1800, the total population of the city included more than 500 slaves and 123 free African Americans. One man, Yarrow Mamout, a devout

▲ *A view of the National Mall at night. The Lincoln Memorial is to the right, the Washington Monument is in the middle, and the Capitol is in the background.*

Muslim, earned his freedom and bought a house in Georgetown in 1800.[3]

▷ Modern African-American Community

Slavery was abolished in Washington, D.C., when the Emancipation Act was signed on April 16, 1862. African Americans began the long journey out of the shadow of slavery after the Civil War. Their battle for lives free from discrimination and prejudice continues.[4] Washington, D.C., has been at the center of that struggle.

These African-American men, dressed in traditional African clothing, are performing in front of the James Buchanan Monument, located in Meridian Hill Park, northeast of the National Mall. According to the 2000 census, African Americans made up 60 percent of the people living in Washington, D.C.

America's first college for African Americans was founded in the federal district in 1867. Howard University became the center of a vibrant intellectual movement that continues today. Many prominent African Americans have received degrees there. In 1868, Sayles Jenks Bowen, a Radical Republican, became the first African-American mayor of Washington, D.C. He advocated integration of the city's separate black and white school systems.

Many African Americans from the deep South migrated to Washington, D.C., between the Civil War and World War I. By 1910, over one hundred thousand African Americans lived in the federal district. Many were America's African-American elite. Six out of every ten citizens in Washington, D.C., today are African American. African Americans play major roles in city culture and government. Many African-American musicians, visual artists, athletes, civil rights activists, business leaders, and government dignitaries were born in the capital or have strong roots there.

Over the course of two centuries, George Washington's city grew from a country village into a proud international city with African-American flair.[5] Aside from being the busy center of government and history, modern Washington, D.C., is a city of neighborhoods. Then and now, it is a doorway to the ideals, the diversity, and the real lives of the American people.

Glossary

civil rights movement—Movement beginning in the 1960s to establish civil rights for African-American citizens.

commerce—The buying and selling of goods on a large scale.

commission—A group of persons responsible for completing a task.

cornerstone—A stone laid in a formal ceremony that forms part of a corner or angle in a wall.

democracy—Form of government in which the people rule through majority voting or by being represented in government by elected officials.

depot—A station where trains or buses load or unload railroad passengers or freight.

encampments—Places where troops have set up camp.

federal district—Section of land set apart as the place from which the central government exercises authority over a federation.

Know-Nothing party—A political group that existed in the 1800s that was fearful of the influence of Catholics and other recent immigrants of the time.

mall—Public area designed as a pedestrian walkway.

mason—Craftsman who builds structures by layering materials such as stone or brick.

memorial—Structure built to keep the memory of a person or event alive (also known as a monument).

obelisk—A four-sided vertical pillar that tapers as it extends upward, ending in a pyramid.

republic—Form of government in which the leader is usually an elected president.

surveyor—Professional who calculates the boundaries and elevation of land.

Chapter 1. A Grand Avenue

1. National Park Service, "We Shall Overcome: Historic Places of the Civil Rights Movement, Lincoln Memorial," n.d., <http://www.cr.nps.gov/nr/travel/civilrights/dc1.htm> (August 17, 2004).

2. The Estate of Martin Luther King, Jr., "Chapter 20: March on Washington," *Martin Luther King Papers Project,* 2002, <http://www.stanford.edu/group/King/publications/autobiography/chp_20.htm> (August 17, 2004).

3. A. Philip Randolph Institute, "Biographical Notes on A. Philip Randolph, 1889–1879," n.d., <http://www.apri.org/Bio-Rand1.htm> (August 17, 2004).

4. Walter Naegle, "Brother Outsider, The Life of Bayard Rustin, 1912–1987," *Bayard Rustin Film Project,* 2002, <http://www.rustin.org/biography.html> (August 17, 2004).

5. The Estate of Martin Luther King, Jr., "Chapter 20: March on Washington."

6. National Park Service, "We Shall Overcome: Historic Places of the Civil Rights Movement."

7. Smithsonian Photographic Services, "Million Man March," *Smithsonian Institution,* 1995, <http://photo2.si.edu/mmm/mmm.html> (August 17, 2004).

8. Kelly Wallace, et al, "'Million Mom March' Puts Gun Control Back in Legislative Firing Line," *CNN,* May 15, 2000, <http://www.cnn.com/2000/US/05/15/million.moms/> (September 2, 2004).

9. Ibid.

Chapter 2. A New Federal City

1. David L. Lewis, *District of Columbia: A Bicentennial History* (New York: W.W. Norton & Company, Inc., 1976), p. 8.

2. Bob Arnebeck, *Through a Fiery Trial: Building Washington 1790–1800* (Latham, Md.: Madison Books, 1991), pp. 11, 13.

3. James Thomas Flexner, *George Washington: Anguish and Farewell* (Boston: Little, Brown and Company, 1972), p. 69.

4. Constance McLaughlin Green, *Washington: Village and Capital, 1800–1878* (Princeton, N.J.: Princeton University Press, 1962), p. 7.

5. Ibid., p. 8.

6. Bernard A. Weisberger, *The District of Columbia* (New York: Time-Life Books, 1996), p. 34.

7. Green, p. 12.

8. Lonnelle Aikman, *We, the People: The Story of the United States Capitol* (Washington, D.C.: The United States Capitol Historical Society, 1978), p. 16.

Chapter 3. America's Front Yard

1. David L. Lewis, *District of Columbia: A Bicentennial History* (New York: W.W. Norton & Company, Inc., 1976), p. 38.

2. Henry Wiencek and Henry Young, *Smithsonian Guides to Historic America: Virginia and the Capital Region* (New York: Stewart, Tabori, & Chang, 1998), p. 44.

3. Donald R. Kennon, *Washington Past & Present: A Guide to the Nation's Capital* (Washington, D.C.: The United States Capitol Historical Society, 1983), pp. 10, 12.

4. Bob Arnebeck, *Through a Fiery Trial: Building Washington 1790–1800* (Latham, Md.: Madison Books, 1991), pp. 43, 56–59, 63, 66–69, 72–82, 85–86, 93–99.

5. Marjorie Ashworth, *Washington, D.C.: A Smithsonian Book of the Nation's Capital* (Washington, D.C.: Smithsonian Books, 1992), p. 73.

6. Arnebeck, pp. 6–8.

7. Lewis, p. 20.

8. National Park Service, "Creation of the National Mall," *National Mall Homepage,* n.d., <http://www.nps.gov/nama/feature/page1.htm> (April 13, 2004).

9. Thomas B. Allen, *The Washington Monument: It Stands for All* (New York: Discovery Books, 2000), p. 46.

10. Wiencek and Young, p. 61.

11. Allen, p. 54.

12. Wiencek and Young, p. 61.

13. Allen, pp. 71–73, 78–79.

14. Ibid., p. 97.

15. National Park Service, "Vietnam Veterans Memorial," April 13, 2004, <http://www.nps.gov/vive/home.htm> (September 2, 2004).

16. National World War II Memorial, "Introduction," 2003, <http://www.wwiimemorial.com/default.asp?page=facts.asp&subpage=intro>, "Facts," <http://www.wwiimemorial.com/archives/factsheets/memorialdesign.htm> (August 23, 2004).

17. National Park Service, "Franklin Delano Roosevelt Memorial," July 11, 2002, <http://www.nps.gov/fdrm/home.htm> (August 22, 2004).

18. National Park Service, "Planning the Memorial," *Thomas Jefferson Memorial,* July 19, 2002, <http://www.nps.gov/thje/memorial/planning.htm> (August 22, 2004); "Building the Memorial," <http://www.nps.gov/thje/memorial/building.htm> (August 22, 2004).

19. National Park Service, "The Cherry Blossoms," May 4, 2004, <http://www.nps.gov/nacc/cherry/indexB.htm> (August 22, 2004).

20. U.S. Army Corps of Engineers, "The Corps' Connection to the Washington, D.C., Tidal Basin and Its Beloved Cherry Trees," *Office of History,* <http://www.hq.usace.army.mil/history/vignettes/Vignette_48.htm> (August 22, 2004).

21. Smithsonian Institution Libraries, "From Smithson to Smithsonian: The Birth of An Institution," January 1998, <http://www.sil.si.edu/Exhibitions/Smithson-to-Smithsonian/intro.html> (April 13, 2004).

22. Ibid.

23. Ibid.

24. National Museum of the American Indian, "About the National Museum of the American Indian," *NMAI in Washington, D.C.,* n.d., <http://www.nmai.si.edu/subpage.cfm?subpage=visitor&second=dc&third=opening> (April 13, 2004).

25. Ibid.

26. Associated Press, "A Statue is Being Dedicated on Veterans Day to the Women Who Served in the Vietnam War. Big Deal? You Bet," 1993.

27. National Capital Planning Commission, "Security and Urban Design," October 2002, <http://www.ncpc.gov/planning_init/security/security.html> (August 25, 2004).

Chapter 4. Jenkins Hill

1. Office of the Curator, "How the Location for the Capitol Was Chosen," *The Architect of the Capitol,* April 2001, <http://www.aoc.gov/cc/capitol/capitol_location.htm> (April 13, 2004).

2. Bob Arnebeck, *Through a Fiery Trial: Building Washington 1790–1800* (Latham, Md.: Madison Books, 1991), p. 63.

3. Gerald R. Gereau, ed. *The Capitol: A Pictorial History of the Capitol and of the Congress, Eighth Edition* (Washington, D.C.: U.S. Government Printing Office, 1981), p. 6.

4. Ibid., p. 7.

5. James Thomas Flexner, *George Washington: Anguish and Farewell* (1793–1799) (Boston: Little, Brown and Company, 1972), p. 88.

6. Lonnelle Aikman, *We, the People: The Story of the United States Capitol* (Washington, D.C.: The United States Capitol Historical Society, 1978), pp. 26–27, 31.

7. Arnebeck, p. 165.

8. Ibid., p. 118.

9. Thomas B. Allen, *The Washington Monument: It Stands for All* (New York: Discovery Books, 2000), p. 7.

10. Jill Ann Duffy and Elizabeth Ardella Laub Lambert, "Homes of the Court," *History of the Court,* 2000, <http://www.supremecourthistory.org/02_history/subs_sites/02_d.html> (April 13, 2004).

11. Ibid.

12. Office of the Curator, "Brief Construction History of the Capitol," *The Architect of the Capitol,* April 2001, <http://www.aoc.gov/cc/capitol/capitol_construction.htm> April 13, 2004.

13. Gereau, p. 17.

14. Ibid., p. 42.

Chapter 5. A Presidential Palace

1. Marjorie Ashworth, *Washington, D.C.: A Smithsonian Book of the Nation's Capital* (Washington, D.C.: Smithsonian Books, 1992), p. 96.

2. Staff, *The White House: An Historic Guide* (Washington, D.C.: White House Historical Association, 1979), p. 106.

3. Ibid.

4. Claire and John Whitcomb, *Real Life at the White House* (New York: Routledge, 2000), p. 5.

5. Wendell Garrett, *The Changing White House* (Boston: Northeastern University Press, 1995), pp. 35, 41.

6. Ashworth, p. 97.

7. Ibid.

8. Ibid., p. 101.

9. Whitcomb, p. xix.

10. Ibid., pp. 15–16.

11. Ibid.

12. Anthony S. Pitch, *The Burning of Washington: The British Invasion of 1814* (Annapolis, Md.: Naval Institute Press, 1998), p. 49.

13. Whitcomb, p. 35.

Chapter 6. The Changing Face of the Federal District

1. Constance McLaughlin Green, *The Secret City: A History of Race Relations in the Nation's Capital* (Princeton, N.J.: Princeton University Press, 1967), pp. 13–15.

2. Marjorie Ashworth, *Washington, D.C.: A Smithsonian Book of the Nation's Capital* (Washington, D.C.: Smithsonian Books, 1992), p. 41.

3. PBS Online, PBS Resource Bank, "Portrait of Yarrow Mamout,"*Africans in America,* 1999, <http://www.pbs.org/wgbh/aia/part2/2h16.html> (August 23, 2004).

4. Sam Smith, "A Short History of Black Washington," *Progressive Review,* n.d., <http://prorev.com/dcblackhist.htm.> (August 23, 2004).

5. Soul of America, "Washington, D.C.: The Arts/Cultural Sites," n.d., <http://www.soulofamerica.com/cityfldr/wash3.html> (April 13, 2004).

Ashabranner, Brent. *On the Mall in Washington, D.C.: A Visit to America's Front Yard.* Brookfield, Conn.: Twenty-First Century Books, 2002.

———. *The New African Americans.* North Haven, Conn.: Linnet Books, 1999.

Curlee, Lynn. *Capital.* New York: Atheneum Books for Young Readers, 2003.

Doherty, Craig A. and Katherine M. Doherty. *The Washington Monument.* Woodbridge, Conn.: Blackbirch Press, 1995.

Dubois, Muriel L. *The Washington Monument.* Mankato, Minn.: Bridgestone Books, 2001.

Haskins, James. *The March on Washington.* New York: HarperCollins Publishers, 1993.

Hilton, Suzanne. *A Capital Capital City: 1790–1814.* New York: Atheneum, 1992.

Johnston, Joyce. *Washington, D.C.* Minneapolis: Lerner Publications, 2003.

Marrin, Albert. *George Washington & the Founding of a Nation.* New York: Dutton Children's Books, 2001.

St. George, Judith. *The White House: Cornerstone of a Nation.* New York: Putnam, 1990.

Stein, R. Conrad. *Washington, D.C.* New York: Children's Press, 1999.

Waters, Kate. *The Story of the White House.* New York: Scholastic, 1991.

A

Adams, Abigail, 36–37
Adams, John, 36–37

B

Bacon, Henry, 22
Banneker, Benjamin, 16, 19, 40
Bowen, Sayles Jenks, 42

C

Capitol building, 12–13, 15, 17, 19–20, 28–33, 37–38, 40–41
Capitol Hill, 18
Cherry Tree Walk, 24–25
civil rights movement, 10–12
Civil War, 19, 22, 27, 33, 41, 42
Congress, 17–19, 30–33, 38, 40
Crawford, Thomas, 33

E

East Potomac Park, 25
Ellicott, Andrew, 16, 19

F

Franklin Delano Roosevelt Memorial, 24
French, Benjamin, 21
French, Daniel Chester, 22

G

George Washington sculpture, 20–21
Greenough, Horatio, 20

H

Hadfield, George, 31
Hallet, Stephen, 29, 31
Hamilton, Alexander, 14
Hoban, James, 31, 35, 38–39
House of Representatives, 30–31

J

Jefferson, Thomas, 14, 19, 24, 28–29, 31, 37, 40
Jefferson Memorial, 20, 24–25
Jenkins Hill, 19, 28–29

K

King, Martin Luther, Jr., 11–12, 27
Know-Nothing party, 21–22
Korean War Veterans Memorial, 23

L

Latrobe, Benjamin, 31
L'Enfant, Pierre Charles, 10, 15–16, 18–19, 28, 31, 34
Lin, Maya, 23
Lincoln, Abraham, 22, 33
Lincoln Memorial, 10–13, 20, 22–23, 41

M

Madison, Dolley, 37
Madison, James, 14, 37–38
McMillan, James, 19–20
McMillan Plan, 19–20
Million Man March, 12
Million Mom March, 12
Mills, Robert, 21
Monroe, James, 36, 38

N

National Museum of the American Indian, 26
National World War II Memorial, 24

O

Olmsted, Frederick Law, Jr., 19, 22

P

Pope, John Russell, 24

R

Rainbow Pool, 22, 24
Reflecting Pool, 22–24
Revolutionary War, 14, 16, 27

S

St. Florian, Friedrich, 24
Senate, 30–31
slavery, 14, 22, 35, 40–41
Smithson, James, 25
Smithsonian Institution, 20, 25–27
Stuart, Gilbert, 37
Supreme Court, 17–19, 30–32
Supreme Court building, 31–33

T

Thornton, William, 29, 31
Tidal Basin, 24–25

U

Ulysses S. Grant Monument, 27
U.S. Botanic Garden, 26–27

V

Vietnam Veterans Memorial, 23

W

Walter, Thomas, 33
War of 1812, 36–38
Washington, George, 10, 14–22, 28–29, 34–37, 40, 42
Washington Monument, 12, 21–22, 24–25, 27, 41
West Potomac Park, 22–24
White House, 15, 17, 19, 28–29, 31, 34–39
Williamson, Collen, 35